Both
SIDES OF THE
Fence

PREACHING AND TEACHING IN ANY CONTEXT

DR JOHNNIE R BRADLEY SR

Sister Highting Thank you for your support

Dr.

outskirts press

Dedication

This book, Both Sides of The Fence: Preaching and Teaching in Any Context is dedicated to God the Father, God the Son and God the Holy Spirit, my wonderful wife DeAndra, and my five wonderful children (Joshua, Jeremiah, Jillian, Johnnie Jr, and Joseph) who has been so supportive of my journey. I have been privileged as well to serve an awesome church: Shiloh Missionary Baptist Church, Dallas, Texas that gives me the flexibility to serve as pastor, preacher, teacher and professor. Along with my various responsibilities I also dedicate this book to Dallas Bible Theological Institute where I serve as president.

I personally thank my Secretary Ann Nance and Academic Dean Dr. Michael Delaney for guarding my time, Lori J., who has been an invaluable help to me through this process; along with Dr. Thomas Spann, Dr. Michael Duduit, Dr. Kris Barnett, and Dr. Tony Matthews.

To God Be The Glory,

Dr. Johnnie R. Bradley Sr.

Pastoral Endorsement

I'm delighted, excited and overjoyed to recommend this book by Dr. Johnnie R. Bradley, Sr. "Both Sides of the Fence: Preaching and Teaching in Any Contexts." My son in the ministry, friend, and fellow laborer in the Gospel of Jesus Christ has written a manuscript to help us bridge the racial divide on Sunday mornings. He has endeavored to accomplish this by providing pastors, preachers and teaches with a homiletical study on the expositional preaching of Dr. E. K. Bailey one of America's finest biblical exegetes'. This book will serve to educate preachers and teaches on the cultural difference in styles of preaching delivery, methods of preparations and the expected call and response in the African American pulpit. If you want to sharpen your study methods, knowledge of preaching and sermon delivery this is a book to help you acquire what you need.

Dr. Terry M. Turner
Senior Pastor of Mesquite Friendship Baptist Church, Mesquite, Texas

It is a joy and a blessing to witness my son-in-law and former understudy, Dr. Johnnie R. Bradley Sr., finish his first published work. With an insatiable appetite for God's word, Dr. Bradley as sought with a passion for the understanding and accuracy of scriptural interpretation. Both Sides of the Fence captures and contextualizes the journey of a preacher who diligently strives to glorify God in his studies and preparation for teaching and preaching. This work also chronologies how his dedication to cut straight the Word of God caused him to transition to expositional teaching and preaching. Both Sides of the Fence captures that exact sentiment in the life of Dr. E K Bailey and demonstrates how to overcome being predictable and succumbing to bias by using their gifts on both sides of the fence. As you read this book you will find key components that will enable you to improve in sermon preparation to impact multi-ethnic crowds.

Pastor Hersey Hammons Jr.
First National Baptist Church, Guthrie, OK

Table of Contents

Foreword

Dr. Thomas W. Spann
Director of the Intern Program
Perkins School of Theology, SMU

African American preaching has been studied from a variety of angles. It has been celebrated as a unique contribution to the advancement of social justice as well as sustaining the cultural and spiritual gifts of Black people. The rhetoric of African American preaching has been highlighted for its poetry, imagery, narrative elements, congregational involvement and passionate delivery. Due to the works of Henry Mitchell and Frank Thomas, the theme of celebration has been the focus of critical and constructive analysis in academic circles. Celebration continues to be practiced in small and large churches as a way of keeping a cultural and a spiritual phenomenon alive and well. However, as a rhetorical expression, it has come under the careful scrutiny of Professor Cleophus LaRue, who, in his book *Rethinking Celebration,* has challenged preachers to rethink the purpose and object of celebration in African American worship.

The author of this book, Dr. Johnnie R. Bradley Sr., is a fine practitioner of the art of celebration in the African American tradition. He, however, has distinguished himself in that he is also a student of the art of preaching. He has read widely; attended numerous conferences on preaching; and has completed the Doctor of Ministry degree at Anderson University. Bradley never tires of talking about preaching.

He is a mentor to many young preachers. He willingly shares his resources to help other preachers to improve. As this book indicates, Bradley is a proponent of a particular type of preaching—not because it is trendy or lucrative, but because of its inherent pedagogical and evangelistic qualities. Bradley lives and breathes expository preaching!

This book records the purpose, power, and possibilities of expository preaching. It is a short but meaningful book on this subject. It offers a brief history of African American preaching, a summary of types of preaching, a definition of expository preaching, and sermonic examples from the late Reverend E. K. Bailey of the Concord Baptist Church in Dallas, Texas. Bradley's treatment of Bailey's journey to claim this type of preaching makes this a worthy read. An analysis of some of Rev. Bailey's sermons provides evidence of how the structure of the sermon and the delivery provided a spiritual blessing to the congregations that heard Bailey's revival sermons. Although hard to capture in print, Bradley worked judiciously to bring forth the spirit and truth of the power of expository preaching in the hands of a master preacher. Moreover, Bradley interviewed Mrs. Sheila Bailey and some of Rev. Bailey's protégés, many of whom are proclaiming the gospel every Sunday using the preaching method taught and modeled by Rev. Bailey.

For preachers who use the expository method, this book says "keep on keeping on!" For those who are contemplating the expository method, this book says "try it; you'll like it." And for those who have not used the expository method, this book says "read, rejoice, and be blessed!"

Introduction

The work that you have in your hands is the expression of a grace-filled, purpose-infused life. To fully step into the material that will be presented, you must first know the journey that I've taken along this process. My life, my studies, my writing, and my ministry all fueled the passion that I have for drawing the church into a deeper love of Scripture.

I was born and raised in Pensacola, Florida and answered a call to preach the Gospel at age 19. My decision to go into the ministry, however, was not a natural progression from the circumstances of my home. Although finances weren't lacking in the early years, my home was often filled with tension and drama because of alcohol and violence. Challenges rose and discouragement existed, but God enabled my family and me to overcome many disparities that hindered our growth.

When I was 9, my dad's anger finally became too much and my parents separated. Our family suffered the consequences. Without his income, my mom, who had not worked in years, was forced back into the job market. She bravely did her best, raising 6 kids and working several jobs. The financial situation was desperate, and while she tried to make the best of a really difficult situation, we spiraled out of control. Without the heavy hand of my father, my siblings and I devolved into very disobedient and disrespectful kids. In retrospect, we made it very hard on my mother.

My escape was sports. I used football, baseball and basketball as a way to distract myself. As a result, I developed a close relationship with my football coach, and on evenings when I couldn't force myself to return home, he opened his house to me. That welcome turned into my second home. For weeks at a time I stayed with my coach and his family. I started adapting to the different culture in his home, appreciating the food, peace, and affluence. It started to change the way I thought and acted, eventually drawing attention to the fact that I was acting differently from my peers and family. I didn't realize how confusing and hurtful this was to my mother. When she feared that she was losing me, she put her foot down and didn't allow me to stay with my coach. As a result, I once again poured myself into sports as a way to push back the tension, suffering and poverty that was at home. At the time, I couldn't imagine a worse environment.

That changed, however, when we moved into Pensacola Village. Pensacola Village was known for being one of the roughest, most violent areas of the city. Finances had gotten so bad that we had to move into this low-income housing. For twelve years my family lived in this area. I was categorized because of where I lived. Disrespect and lack of ambition threatened to kill any dreams I had of making something of myself. I started skipping school. I started drinking. I lost my love for sports. I started listening to those around me who said that I would never amount to anything, even predicting that, because of the bad choices I was consistently making, I wouldn't live to the age of 25.

For the longest time, I listened to those voices. Sometimes, people's opinions pulled me under. Sometimes, my stubbornness fought to prove them wrong. All the while, my mom was praying for me. My Uncle Johnny and Aunt Vera Newton took me to church on occasion, and I remember Pastor Otha Leverette Sr., at St. John Divine Missionary Baptist Church, preaching colorful messages. All of this settled on the inside of me, even when my exterior and actions looked anything but godly. One Sunday, while attending Covenant Christian Ministries, I gave my heart to God. I accepted Christ as my personal savior and put my life in His hands.

As I hungered to learn about my renewed faith, I poured myself into the church. New Covenant Christian Ministries was a new non-denominational church led by Ross O. Knight Jr. He started the church with five recovering alcoholics and three recovering cocaine users. The church had a highly-structured approach to ministry, and that was exactly what I needed. I jumped into the study of the Word with a great amount of passion, and after a committed time in worship, prayer and consistency, I made a 360-degree turnaround.

The next stage of life for me was college, and I attended the University of Southern Mississippi with a dream to play football for them. I was accepted on the team as a walk-on, although I never really saw any game time. While I spent my energy trying to create a successful sports career, God was trying to get my attention. I was in my dorm room in Bond Hall at USM when I heard the Lord's voice tell me to return home to Pensacola and begin working with my home church, St. John Divine Missionary Baptist Church. Going back home was hard, but good for me. While I truly had received Christ earlier in my life, I had strayed from what I had been taught. I wasn't living according to Scripture and I had stumbled into making bad decisions. Once again, in the structure that helped me to thrive, I was became settled, focused and changed inwardly. It was at this church that I received my call to preach.

Shortly after this shift in priorities and focus, I met my wife. We dated, married and moved to her home state of Oklahoma. In Oklahoma, the Lord blessed me with several mentors for the various facets of my life. The common thread of advice I received from them was that I should attend seminary. They believed in the call on my life and knew that I needed to develop my mind for God's use. In response to that counsel, my wife and I journeyed to Dallas, Texas to study at Dallas Baptist University, where I received a Bachelor of Science degree and a Master of Arts degree. I also completed additional module studies in Expository Preaching at Faith Evangelical Seminary on Tacoma, Washington, and most recently I received a Doctorate of Ministry degree in Expository Preaching from Anderson University in Anderson, South Carolina.

One of the things birthed through my education process was a desire to explore how servant leadership could be utilized in the local church to further God's kingdom. Before being called to pastor where I presently minister, I served as Associate Pastor to three senior pastors in Florida, Oklahoma and Texas. At their feet, I learned to serve well and gained the practical experience necessary to lead a congregation of my own. In August of 2006, I accepted a position as Senior Pastor of Shiloh Missionary Baptist Church in Dallas, Texas where I've had the privilege of leading an amazing congregation. In 2012, I was elected to serve as the president of Dallas Bible Theological Institute. DBTI trains men and women to be servant leaders in their local church and community. Through these positions, I hope to have an eternal impact with the message of hope through the Word of God.

I also recognize that helping the church remain relevant in the 21st century is not possible if she utilizes 18th century methods. I spent a large focus of my education studying how spiritual formation, expository preaching/teaching and Christian education should be used to equip the local church for ministry (Ephesians 4:11 – 13). I believe that there is a great impact to be felt when passionate preachers around the nation employ these methods. Well-rounded preparation allows preachers to deliver an accurate and compelling gospel message to a fallen humanity. Being able to preach in multi-ethnic settings and being proficient in expository methods are keys to reaching all people through the Gospel. If the only tools in a preacher's toolbox are based on systems developed during a different era and for reasons that are no longer applicable, then the effectiveness of his preaching will be hindered.

Accepting Jesus Christ changed the whole trajectory of my life. I went from a lost, hopeless, and rebellious kid with no hope for a pleasant future, to a redeemed, loved and passionate man who dreams of having a positive impact on the body of Christ. My focus has become learning and serving, and I've been blessed to have had ample opportunity to do both. I've fed the hungry, clothed the needy and visited the sick – all of which I once was. I am greatly humbled when I am able to be a blessing to those who are in poverty, who are less fortunate, and who are in unfair positions. It was through the preaching ministry where my life turned to assist in the cause of Christ. That is why Jesus came: to seek and save that which is lost. My greatest asset is being saved by the blood of Christ, and I credit all my success in life and ministry to my loving heavenly Father.

CHAPTER 1

Emergence of Expository Preaching

THERE IS A countless amount of good that happens on a Sunday morning around this nation. People's lives are being transformed, God's name is being lifted and honored, and parishioners are being challenged and inspired. Some systems are in place that help pastors in their goals of imparting truth and life to their congregation. As with all systems, however, if we forget how and why they are developed, it is not long before we are following patterns that have strayed far from the cause they were intended to serve. One of those systems is the style in which preaching is accurately done.

There is a story of a young lady and her friend who were preparing a roast in the kitchen. Her friend noticed that before she put the roast in the pan, she cut both ends off. Her friend asked her why. She said, "I don't really know. That is the way mom always prepared it." The next time she was with her mom, she asked her mom how she prepared a roast. At the end of her mom's explanation, she added, "And then you cut both ends off." The young lady asked her mom why she did that, and she answered, "Well, my mom always prepared her roast this way. You should ask her." The young lady called her grandma and asked how she made a pot roast. After a description of the spices and processes used, she concluded with, "And then you cut both ends off." "Why did you do that, grandma?" the young lady asked. Her grandma reflected for a minute and then replied, "Well, the pan the roast went in was smaller than the roast. I had to cut the ends off to get the roast to fit in the pan."

Some of our behaviors and systems were created long ago. It is helpful to occasionally revisit these systems to see if they're still serving our needs, or to examine why we are still using them when there is a better option available to us. *Why* we do things is the foundation for *what* we do. If we fail to look at the reasons behind our decisions, we might fail to achieve the goals for which we're striving. It seems obvious to say, but just because it worked for those who went before us doesn't mean it is the most efficient, effective way to do it today.

Preaching, in its ideal form, is used to convey the overall message of the Bible, heralding the message that the Holy Spirit has given to the preacher, while proclaiming the declaratory announcements grounded in Scripture itself. Powerful and uplifting preaching has never been an issue within the African American community. Historical evidence abounds in churches, books, conventions and conversations with those who have witnessed, listened to and celebrated the craft. There are primarily four types of preaching styles: *exhortative, textual, exegetical and expositional.* Of the four primary types of preaching, expositional preaching is identified as the most text-centric. Indeed, one of the defining qualities of the African American church is Christian preaching; the form, the power, and the authority are well known. For the African American church, early methods of preaching relied heavily upon emotional appeals and were short on exegesis. Unfortunately, this tradition continues for some. Sound text-based exploration and explanation of Scriptures is not exercised in all churches, particularly black churches.

This is a story about the black church in America, preaching styles utilized on a weekly basis, and a strong, Godly leader who modeled a new way of studying and communicating God's Word. It is hoped that by revisiting the history of the African American church and introducing this audience to a genuinely transformative leader, it will cause the church to look at her methods in a different light and communicate more in multi-ethnic settings. In the right hands, this book will be a magnifying glass for multi-ethic churches that allows us to study the why and how of communicating the Gospel on a weekly basis. It is my hope that this book is a catalyst for reflection, analyzation, and modification for pastors/preachers evaluating their preaching and teaching.

CHAPTER 2

Case for Biblical Exposition

AFRICAN AMERICAN PREACHING is categorized differently from other forms of preaching because the practice and manner of engagement in preaching differs greatly from other ethnicities that also proclaim the Gospel. Clearly, African American preaching is not the only type of acceptable preaching, but simply differs from other preaching forms. The value of this form of preaching has never been diminished or marginalized, regardless of cultural transitions that have occurred. To look at the present model of church and style of preaching traditionally utilized within a modern African American church, it is helpful to study from where these styles and traditions originated. Present preaching models and the way a congregation responds to sermons did not spring suddenly into existence, but rather were developed during a long, difficult, and often disconnected series of events related to slavery and oppression. This is an attempt to create a thread of understanding of the way in which black preaching and oral traditions were adapted during a time when documentation was minimal.

The earliest records of African American church history began during slavery. Throughout this period, for the most part, the spiritual lives of slaves were ignored. There were a few missionaries who attempted to reach out to them, but owners and the church often stepped in to limit this effort. Fear propelled the idea that, if slaves learned about the freedom expressed in the Gospel, there would be an expectation for freedom in their lives. Even if a slave owner believed that the behavior of their slaves would be better if they were evangelized, preachers were instructed to limit the topics preached to ones that talked about obedience and duty, trying to create moral humans. Being excluded from formal education, slaves had a hard time participating in a religious system that relied on Latin and highly intricate hierarchies and creeds.

Even though any gathering of slaves was a concern to slave owners, African Americans found ways to gather and express their faith. Occasionally slaves heard sermons from itinerate white preachers; however, the practice of having black ministers preach to their own people became more common as time went on. During slavery and reconstruction, when African Americans could not write their names, could not understand business nor understand the importance of education, when they were not allowed to display that knowledge even if they possessed it, Christian preaching was their lens of understanding. Oral culture (messages or testimony verbally transmitted in speech or song) and extemporaneous sermons (impromptu speeches given without any preparation) were how social and religious information was conveyed.[1]

In the harshest of times, the preached Word aided in reducing pain, suffering and anxiety that was in response to all manner of societal ills directly and indirectly related to slavery. African American preaching provided hope during even the bleakest of times. The church established itself as the greatest source of community, religious education, and social development. Preaching was the primary vehicle to accomplish this.

In the mid-18th century, America experienced a great outpouring of religious enthusiasm. The Great Awakening, as it was called, inspired an expressive reinvigoration of spiritual fervor that resonated with the emotive religious expressions of faith brought from West Africa.[2] While this wave of spirituality was slightly more inclusive than the pious religiosity that had been expressed before, most of the enslaved were still excluded from traditional churches. Two of the foremost leaders of the movement, Jonathan Edwards and George Whitefield, were slave owners themselves. The revivalists generally did not challenge slavery, but they did preach to everyone regardless of race. While the Great Awakening lacked the support to eradicate slavery, it laid the foundation for substantive conversations regarding abolition.

By the late 18th century, blacks had begun to gather in associations called African Societies. Straddling the line between religious organizations and self-help groups, they were the birth place of the first independent black churches. In 1787, Richard Allen and Absalom Jones created and gave structure to the Free African Society of Philadelphia. This organization later evolved into Bethel Church, the mother church of the African Methodist Episcopal (AME) denomination, and St. Thomas Episcopal Church, which remained affiliated with a white Episcopal denomination.[3] They created relationships with similar groups in other cities, and the movement spread.

Even in the early 1800s, preaching played a significant role in the abolitionist movement. In the first three decades of the nineteenth century, written material, such as speeches, sermons or newspapers, were scarce.[4] The inclusion of early sermons in African American literature creates greater understanding as to the roots of African American literary culture. Early African American literature tends to focus on Phyllis Wheatley, Frederick Douglass and David Walker. Documented sermons represent a continuous stream of African American literature that bridge the eighteenth and nineteenth centuries.[5] Early sermons spoke to the depressing condition of the slaves and gave blacks an opportunity to express themselves through Scripture by sharing social justice metaphors found throughout the Bible.

During this time, the narrative form of communication was the primary vehicle used in the African American church. As preachers began to develop their unique styles of communicating, stories were a natural part of sermons. Even black literature mimicked this style of narration found in preaching. Narrative communication typically lacked the cultural, grammatical, and literary study in the preparation and preaching of the text; however, biblical narratives told a story that could connect to the heart of the listener while at the same time emphasize the underlying point of the text. Born out of oral tradition, narratives are still an important part of the African American preacher's repertoire.

As the nation approached civil war, the black church found its voice in the cause of abolition. African American preachers spoke out against slavery. With boldness, they cautioned that any nation that tolerated slavery would suffer divine punishment, and to back up their words, they joined white abolitionists in organizing the Underground Railroad. After emancipation, black churches became a place for African Americans to find refuge. Education, denied them during slavery, became a priority to newly freed slaves. They pooled their resources to buy land to erect their own churches and schools. For many years, the black church doubled as a community center. During the era of the Jim Crow laws, it became an independent institution with black leadership.

Following the abolishment of slavery, the way in which preachers prepared and communicated started to evolve towards exhortation preaching. Exhortation preaching gives congregants a way to interact with the message being conveyed, providing additional hope to the population.[6] This form of preaching, also referred to as call and response, was commonly used at the time. If done correctly, it can increase the engagement level of the congregation. In theory, if the congregants are required to actively participate in the sermon, they become more attentive, which in turn increases biblical knowledge and comprehension of the message being conveyed.[7] Parishioners may be asked to respond with a noise, a word, a phrase, or some other variant, ensuring that the parishioners are engaged with the sermon. Unfortunately, while parishioners may appear to be engaged with the sermon, engagement is not necessarily an indicator of what, if anything, is being learned.

Other races have traditionally viewed African American sermons negatively because of the emotion and zeal expressed. Although amazed at the methods of delivery used, many audiences did not recognize or respect the depth of the African American sermon. According to Dr. Henry Mitchell, when African American preachers started to receive formal training in newly accredited schools, African American preaching came into its own and began to be viewed as a serious movement. This formal education introduced multiple forms of preaching, such as textual, exegetical and expository.

During the Civil Rights era, Black churches played a primary role in protests. By this time, they were well established as community and political bases, and often people gathered in crowded church classrooms to develop mobilization plans. Even the marches took on the personality of a Sunday morning service by utilizing prayers and church songs. And, of course, on August 28, 1963, a pastor named Martin Luther King, Jr., preached one of the most famous speeches of the 20th century, "I Have a Dream." In this speech, he used the language of Scripture and paired it with political documents, such as the Constitution and the Declaration of Independence, to remind everyone of the verbiage of social justice and equality the founding fathers implemented.[8]

As far as present-day racism, America is still very far behind what it should be. There are key issues that remain entirely unchanged. As a result, increasing numbers of African Americans are looking for answers from their pastors and from theology. The African American church remains a source of strength. At the same time, there is a trend towards increased diversity within the church. Within the mega-church model, predominately white congregations have attracted significant numbers of African Americans, and predominately black churches are finding people of other races coming to join them to worship together. African American churches have made connections to the larger Christian community and serve people of all races.

As this era finds its place in history, the story that will be told of the African American church will undoubtedly include the church's role in the persistent struggle for civil rights, the advancement of technology and how that has affected the church, and the development of new models of church that better serve a new generation. The African American church is working out a delicate balance between honoring the old traditions, while at the same time utilizing biblical preaching that addresses African American core concerns.

CHAPTER **3**

African American Preaching Emerges with a Multi-Ethnic Approach

POWERFUL AND UPLIFTING preaching has never been an issue within the African American community. Historical evidence abounds in churches, books, conventions and conversations with those who have witnessed, listened to and celebrated the craft.[9] Indeed, one of the defining qualities of the African American church is preaching; the form, the power, and the authority are well known. Within the context of African American churches, preaching is intrinsic, unique and valuable, serving as a beacon to the African American community for generations.

According to Dr. O. C. Edwards, who authored the book *History of Preaching*, there is no activity more characteristic of the church than preaching. Edwards says, "Along with the sacraments, most Christian bodies consider proclamation of the Word of God to be the constitutive act of the church. No other religion gives preaching quite the central role that it has in Christianity. Most major religions authorize persons to ritualize and storify their integrating myths, to preserve, interpret, and teach current relevance to their sacred writings, but the preacher in Christianity plays a more central role."[10]

In his book *Between Two Worlds,* the late theologian and author John R.W. Stott argues that the preacher is suspended between earth and heaven.[11] I would suggest that the African American preacher is between far more than just two worlds. It may be argued that the African American preacher is suspended between four worlds: heaven and earth, as Stott describes, but also between the harsh past and the liberated present. As a result of this unique position, as well as the juxtaposition of the African American preacher at the crossroads of reality and eternity, past and present, the preacher serves as both the message and the messenger. It may further be argued that the harsh past of the African American population, in conjunction with the liberated present, is represented by Stott's heaven and earth. The African American preacher's life is framed by the challenges of his ancestors. Understanding this affirmation provides insight into the manner in which content may be addressed and perceived within the confines of the sermon itself.

Most the time, the African American preacher has excelled at meeting the needs of the congregation served. In the African American church, the preacher teaches, preaches, counsels, conducts business meetings, provides pastoral care and mentors individuals within his congregation and in the community at large. The African American preacher is available to his congregation, which allows him to be more informed about the inner workings of the community, enabling the messages being delivered from the pulpit to be in alignment with the needs of the people. This ensures that the messages are relevant, fresh and provide insights that may be used in their lives. In other words, the preacher is more than just a preacher. He is an accessible servant of God whose purpose is to attend to the needs of the church and its congregants. Preaching the Word of God is an anchor, providing stability to the African American community and playing a tremendous role in the progression, development, and maturity of the community as a whole.

According to Mitchell, preaching in the black church is different than other types of preaching among other ethnicities.[12] This is partly a result of the forms of preaching employed. The practice and manner of engagement for African American preaching differs greatly from other nationalities and races that also proclaim the Gospel. African American preachers are working to increase the knowledge base from which they operate; however, criticism continues regarding the presentation used in their teaching and preaching. As we stated earlier, during the times of slavery and Jim Crow, African Americans were unlearned in many areas; such is not the case today. There are many opportunities for individuals of all races, creeds and religions to be informed, instructed and encouraged toward greatness through exposition of Scripture. When preaching in the African American context, many preachers add more pictures and stories to the content to ensure the congregation grasps the meaning of the message. Many ministers employ all the drama and poetry at their command, inserting imagery into their biblical accounts.

Although the form in which the message is delivered is altered for understanding, the preacher should never lose sight of the goal, which is to communicate the Gospel effectively. The message that is being preached should not be used solely as a means of exciting emotions, but should serve as a means of educating the listener and transforming the listener's heart to draw the congregation into a closer relationship with God. Such a task may be accomplished through careful consideration of the content in the message. If a preacher is thorough and efficient in his preparation, the content of the message should not change, regardless of the form employed by the preacher.

Expositional preaching works to explain the original meaning of a given biblical text. It allows the preacher to inform the mind, instruct the heart and influence the behavior of the congregation toward godliness.[13] This particular form of preaching is important because it conveys God's message to man, providing an opportunity for the listener to be redeemed through a positive response to the Gospel. Phillips Brooks, who authored the book *Lectures on Preaching*, indicates that this type of preaching is like truth that is being poured through a human personality and used to transform lives.[14]

The Emergence of Expository Preaching

If an individual were to conduct a search on "expository preaching, teaching conferences and workshops" on Google, over 41,000 web responses would be generated. Churches offer expository preaching and teaching workshops, and seminaries and Bible schools offer courses on expository preaching. There are even several individual ministries that offer annual conferences highlighting this preaching form. Expository preaching has been a recognized form of preaching for more than a century; however, within the last 30 years, several well-known biblical teachers and preachers have worked to further promote the expository preaching movement. Rev. E.K. Bailey worked tirelessly and effectively to bring the expository preaching style to the African American church. Even still, there are many African American churches throughout the country failing to help their parishioners experience full spiritual growth and life-changing preaching that the expository form can bring. The church is making progress in communicating truth through exposition, but improvement is vital to ensuring that the highest levels of spiritual growth are attained.

In the communication of truth, expositional preaching enables the preacher to say what God says, removing personal opinion from the mixture. Many sermons are losing their Biblical authority because they mix their own opinions in with the preaching of the Word. In the admirable push to connect and be relevant, the content of the message can suffer. Sermons should be informative, insightful, interesting, challenging, convincing, and most of all, accurate. Greg Heisler, author and theologian, contends, "You may be able to change a person's mind for the moment, but only the Spirit of God through exposition can change his/her heart for all eternity through preaching of the Gospel."[15] When preachers focus on expositional preaching, it enables them to construct a message that effectively penetrates the heart and mind of the listener.

Progress towards improving biblical literacy is slow. Ed Stetzer, church planter and Christian Missiologist, states that "America can be proud of many things: our innovation, generosity and entrepreneurial spirit are unsurpassed. Yet when it comes to our nation understanding one of the greatest gifts ever given to humanity – the Bible – we're moving away from the same."[16] People are aware of the basic content of the Bible, but that knowledge does not translate to creating meaning in their lives. It is essential to explore the question of whether current practices in preaching are enabling congregants to become more knowledgeable regarding the Bible.

Local churches are tasked with communicating with individuals and leading them to Christ. Such a course of action cannot occur if there is not an effective plan in place to ensure that individuals understand the Gospel. To address this matter, I propose that local churches should embrace expository preaching, giving parishioners the opportunity to understand the Bible in a simplistic way that is easy to comprehend. Although expository preaching was not traditionally a widely-used method of preaching, as early as 1903 the term "expository sermon" was in printed publications to describe homiletical discourse.[17] The practice of employing the expository form of preaching is one that has served churches well over the years. For decades, books and theological researchers have lauded the benefits of expository preaching. It is through the Word that preaching can meet the needs of the people.

Expositional preaching differs from other types of preaching. It connects, corrects, and corrals the preacher, requiring him to stay tied to the text throughout the course of the sermon. Haddon Robinson, the father of expository preaching stated, "Expository preaching is the communication of a biblical concept, derived from and transmitted through a historical, grammatical, literary study of a passage in its context, which the Holy Spirit first applies to personality and experience of the preacher, then through him to his learners."[18] Expository preaching does not compromise content for form. The expository preacher does not compromise the message to increase the number of individuals joining the church, nor to increase his personal status.

Preaching and the Bible

The messages contained within the Bible do not vary with the passage of time. They remain constant, ever-present, simply waiting for the appropriate attention to be placed upon them. The message is intrinsic and valuable. The preacher is responsible, at least in part, if they fail to provide the congregation the knowledge necessary to make the appropriate choice regarding their actions. As 2 Timothy 3:16 states, "All Scripture is given by inspiration of God, and is profitable for doctrine, for reproof, for correction, for instruction in righteousness, that the man of God may be complete, thoroughly equipped for every good work." G.W. Knight tells us, "The reminder of Timothy's long acquaintance with the scriptures and their central function leads Paul to conclude this section with a more robust statement on the divine origin and specific usefulness of scripture and on the purpose that it serves in the life of the man of God. Scripture from the Bible is interpreted as God-Breathed. Many different nuances in regards to God-Breathed, but one thing is understood and that is when God-breathes the Scripture it is profitable and has a way of correcting any person that is willing to submit to the Word of God."[19]

Scripture is profitable and can accomplish what God has intended to accomplish in the lives of people. It is through the foolishness of preaching the Scriptures (1 Corinthians 1:21) that God breathes correction, change and consistency. This helps to shape how people approach situations in their lives. Out of all that is proclaimed, man receives what God has allowed the preacher to speak. The Scripture is provided by God and is fit for teaching, for explaining which actions should be avoided, for revealing which actions need correction, and for serving as a means of instructing the individual on how he should conduct himself within a given situation. In 2 Timothy 3:15, Paul had just written that the Scriptures can make one wise regarding salvation, a lesson Timothy had learned long before. Timothy's mother and grandmother had a large influence on him, and that influence contributed to him learning the Scriptures (2 Timothy 1:5). Paul knew Timothy had been groomed by his family, and he wanted to reemphasize the crucial role of God's inscripturated revelation in his present ministry.

Paul placed heavy burdens of ministry on his young disciple in this letter; however, he didn't do so irresponsibly. He was confident of Timothy's commitment to, and dependence on, the Scriptures. He was even more confident of God's ability to supply all Timothy's needs through the Word. In the first epistle, Timothy joined Paul and served on the evangelistic team. After discipling, teaching and training Timothy, Paul sent him to Ephesus. In the second epistle, Paul gave Timothy both an assignment and farewell instructions as he reminded him to stay focused on preaching the Word of God. Although this epistle was written while he was incarcerated, Paul wanted to make sure Timothy understood that, whether bound or free, exposition of the scriptures was essential. Paul's goal as Timothy's mentor was to convey the understanding that ministers should not shirk the responsibility of sharing the Word of God.

Paul also instructs Timothy, in 2 Timothy 2:16, that as he teaches Scripture, he must "shun profane and idle babble for they will increase to more ungodliness." This means that the message the Holy Spirit gives the preacher should be conveyed with clarity. The message should not deviate on a tangent nor confuse the listener. The sermon should clearly illuminate the text and should present the message in a way that can be understood, regardless of biblical literacy, age or level of education. In I Corinthians, Paul presents the same information about preaching and the message. "These things we also speak, not in words which man's wisdom teaches but which the Holy Spirit teaches, comparing spiritual things with spiritual. But the natural man does not receive the things of the Spirit of God, for they are foolishness to him; nor can he know them, because they are spiritually discerned." (1 Corinthians 2:13-14)

God, through His sovereign wisdom, uses preaching to transform unbelievers and to strengthen believers. It is the responsibility of the preacher to provide the understanding of the Word of God through the sermon, presenting the message so that others may acquire more insight into God's Word. The preacher knows that "Christ did not send (him) to baptize but to preach the gospel, and not with wisdom of words, lest the cross of Christ should be made of no effect. For the message of the Cross is foolishness to those who are perishing, but to us who are being saved it is the power of God." (1 Corinthians 1:17-18) The purpose of preaching is not simply to baptize additional individuals, nor is it to attempt to appear smarter or more knowledgeable than the congregation. Instead, it is to present the Word of God in a manner that is honest, open and informational. In 1 Corinthians 9:16, Paul emphatically expresses his feelings about his call to preach by declaring, "Woe to me if I do not proclaim the gospel."

For most, salvation does not come without preaching, and baptism comes only as the sequel to the response of faith after hearing the message. Paul was trained by Gamaliel, a well-respected scholar, he understood the rabbinical law and he was intellectually astute. Even still, he wanted those believers at Corinth to understand that only Christ, not wisdom or intellect, could offer a salvific response. Redemption only comes when exposition is crafted to uplift Jesus Christ. Therefore, the preacher should not set himself as better than or above the congregation. He should instead preach to his congregants as equals, presenting the message of the sermon in a relevant and comprehendible manner that will still convey all necessary information.

The individual should preach faithfully that which is written. In I Corinthians 1:21, Paul exemplified the importance of preaching the Gospel, as well as echoing the same message to his son, Timothy. As 2 Timothy 4:2 states, the preacher should, "Preach the word! Be ready in season and out of season. Convince, rebuke, exhort, with all long-suffering and teaching. For the time will come when they will not endure the sound doctrine, but according to their own desires, because they have itching ears, they will heap up for themselves teachers; and they will turn their ears away from the truth, and be turned aside to fables. But you be watchful in all things, endure afflictions, do the work of an evangelist, fulfill your ministry." These verses are overflowing with commands written as *imperatives,* which simply means that you do not have an option - this is something you must do.

Paul gave Timothy directions to preach the Word. Timothy had to do something that was not popular and that might even be dangerous—he had to be ready to proclaim the Gospel and ready to confront the erroneous teachings of individuals in the church. Paul also challenged Timothy to hold strong to the Word of God. In 1 Timothy 4: 3-4, Timothy was instructed to have patience, to teach, instruct, confront, rebuke and exhort believers in the Body of Christ. Paul's instructions to Timothy are profitable to the church as God's Word is timeless.[20] The Bible states that individuals will turn away, preferring fables to the truth; however, if the Word is preached strong and true, the individual will be persuaded to listen, staying on the path of righteousness and away from an ungodly path.

One of the most important questions a preacher should contemplate is how to best apply the practices and lessons from the Bible into his ministry. He has two basic choices on how to convey his message through his preaching: to use exposition, or to decline to use exposition. In order to determine which preaching form to employ, and which of these forms may best serve the purpose of the preacher, specifically the ministry to the people, it becomes necessary to understand what is and what is not classified as exposition.

What is Exposition?

Exposition is defined as "the act of explaining something; a setting forth of the meaning or purpose (as of a writing); discourse or an example of it designed to convey information or explain what is difficult to understand."[21] When applied to the matter of preaching, "expository preaching is the communication of a biblical concept, derived from and transmitted through a historical, grammatical, and literary study of a passage in its context, which the Holy Spirit first applies to the personality and experience of the preacher, then through him to his hearers."[22]

Perhaps the most important aspect of expository preaching is that the information does not come from the preacher. The knowledge and information provided by the preacher must come from within the text itself. The same holds true for the authority wielded by the preacher.

While this may seem like a small distinction, it is an important one. The preacher is meant to assist the congregation in understanding the Word of God. Creating an expository sermon is a multi-step process. The preacher must first read and understand the text, asking himself several questions throughout the process to gain a better understanding of what he hopes to say, what the message of the text is, and how he should present the information. To do this, the preacher must rigorously study the passage. Next, he must take that information and tease out the meaning contained therein, gaining a basic idea of the message being presented in that passage. The purpose of the sermon should become clear through this process, allowing the preacher to create an outline of the message that he is starting to see form in his mind. Once the outline is complete, the basics of the sermon may be filled in. The entire process may be expounded upon through explanation of the text and elimination of extraneous concepts, thus ensuring that the message and meaning of the passage is made clear.

Richard Mayhue, the Vice President and Dean of The Master's Seminary and a Professor of Pastoral Ministries, has attempted to clarify both what constitutes and what does not constitute expository preaching. When speaking of what constitutes expository preaching, he refers to the authenticity of Biblical preaching itself. A sermon must focus on God's revelation, as opposed to what man, or more specifically, the preacher, may find personally significant in the Bible. Mayhue argued that if "a return to true biblical exposition does not occur, and if the church does not return to true biblical preaching... the western world would continue its descent toward a valueless culture."[23]

Expository preaching requires that the preacher proclaim God's word, that he explain to the congregation the power of the message, and that he present enough information that the individual within the congregation may take the lessons learned from the Bible and apply those lessons to his own life. The message is already present within the text. In expository preaching, it is the responsibility of the preacher to simply convey that message, and not what he thinks that the text may mean. The preacher explains, illustrates and offers examples of applying the message.

There are six primary qualities present in expository preaching.[24] Each of these qualities has its own expressed meaning through which a clearer picture of exposition may be formed.

1. Intended Meaning "In expository preaching the preacher's first aim is to discover the text writer's intended theological meaning in the selected text."[25] In order to ensure that this quality is present within the sermon, the preacher must gain an exact understanding of the text, or passage within the text, through careful study of the passage and the content contained therein. Ramesh Richard, in his work *Scripture Sculpture: A Do It Yourself Manual for Biblical Preaching*, calls this first area the flesh of the passage.[26] The fundamental process of studying the text enables preachers to find the keys to the text. It lays the groundwork for serious study in accurately seeing and seeking what the Bible desires to communicate to all people.

2. Intended Message The second quality of expository preaching demands "that the preacher let the text speak through the sermon with the same theological message."[27] The preacher must take the message of the text, in its original language, and translate the same message without embellishment. This message should be conveyed in common language to ensure that the audience is able to clearly understand and identify the purpose of the message and the contextual meaning thereof. In his book *Making of the Sermon* by T. Hardwood Pattison, he writes that the text should govern the sermon. The text is the subject matter of the sermon, and it should be treated with no intention of misuse in understanding the verbiage, the meaning, and the theme that the original author is conveying. The preacher must be conscientious about what the text is communicating.[28]

3. Intended Analysis The third quality of expository preaching is that the preacher using the expository method discovers the meaning of the text through a careful exegetical analysis of the text.[29] This refers to the practice of examining each word within the passage to determine the exact meaning. This should be done while examining the specific context used within the given passage of text. All nuances and details present within the text must be examined to ensure that the message being presented is equal to the message present within the text, without personal bias in the interpretation. Identifying the meaning of the words allows the preacher to understand what the text is saying in its context and culture. When the text is approached with clarity, it allows the preacher to be able to understand any expressions that exist within the message of the text.

4. Original Context The fourth quality of expository preaching dictates that careful consideration of the original contexts in which the text was written must occur in the exploration of the text itself.[30] In order to ensure that the appropriate message is being presented exactly as conveyed through the text, the preacher must have an understanding of the society and the culture as it was during the time the text was written. The meanings of words and the expressions used vary throughout the ages, causing the message to have the potential to become obfuscated, lost to time or conveyed improperly. This can happen if the appropriate knowledge base is not present for application to the text itself. Differences in the translation of the text and the presence of regional variations serve to further compound the matter, making it that much more of an exacting process needed to tease out the original meaning and original message behind the words themselves. William Evans, in his work *How to Prepare Sermons,* stated that the preacher must understand the historical manners and customs that are involved in a text.[31] For example, the Jews wore certain types of garments and had rules and regulations that governed their society. The knowledge of historical culture allows the preacher to paint a holistic picture of a particular text.

5. Structural Integrity "An expository sermon is organized with due consideration to the structure and genre of the selected passage."[32] A preacher must, in his presentation of the information within the passage or passages, consider the manner in which the original writer constructed the text.

6. Faith Enhancing The last quality of expository preaching indicates that expository preaching should aim for the congregation to respond in faith and obedience to the biblical truth. Taking into account all the previous qualities or criteria, the sermon must also work to fulfill, enhance or increase the overall faith of the individual. Sermons must convey a relevant message of God's Word to the congregation; however, the message conveyed must also draw each individual listener into the presence of God. The Bible guides believers to truth, and one of the primary goals of expository preaching is to see James 1:22 (doers of the Word and not hearers only) lived out in the life of every believer. "The distinctive characteristic of expository preaching is its instructional function. An explanation of the details of a given text imparts information that is otherwise unavailable to the average untrained parishioner and provides him with a foundation for Christian growth and service."[33]

Expository preaching serves to create a total experience for the listener with a multi-layered purpose. Each segment of the sermon must be crafted in such a way as to ensure that all six components of expository preaching are present within the context of the message. If this is expository preaching, this begets the question as to what is not expository preaching.

What is Not Exposition?

It is perhaps easier to identify what does not count as exposition than it is to clearly elucidate what does. Any form of preaching or any sermon that does not include the six basic tenets of expository preaching is considered to be a form other than expository preaching. If the message is presented from the perspective of the preacher, or if it is based on the relevance that the preacher finds within the text as opposed to the exact message of the text, then this sermon would not qualify as expository preaching. If the message has an external agenda, such as vainglory that is designed to benefit man as opposed to glorifying God, the message is not an expository one. The ultimate goal is for the preacher to glorify God and find relevance in the text.

Biblical exposition has been shown, through both presentation and comparison, to be the superior preaching form for implementation within the African American church. Not only does this form of preaching work to ensure that the biblical literacy of the congregation is improved, it also works to ensure that the Word of God is made relevant within the congregation. The Book becomes not just a book, but the Living Word, providing meaning and application to daily life. At the same time, it serves as a vessel through which the average person can collect and retain the knowledge that he needs to ensure a high level of faith and spirituality.

A case for biblical exposition through a review and analysis of the selected verses and passages found in the Bible supports the benefit of such a preaching form. It is not enough to simply understand what expository preaching is. In order to understand the reasons that expository preaching should be implemented on a larger scale within the African American community, it must be understood how this form of preaching solves a given need within the community.

CHAPTER **4**

African American Preaching Forms

THE AFRICAN AMERICAN church was, and still is, the anchor of the black community. Not only does it provide an arena for political and educational activities, it has given birth to social activism and spiritual renewal. Central to this great institution is the preacher and his unique style. Samuel Proctor writes, "No one in society has as much responsibility as the preacher for altering our perception of the world around us from that of a chemical-physical accident to the handiwork of a loving, caring God."[34]

The four preaching forms that we will examine are exegetical, exhortation, textual and expository. When looking at these different preaching forms, it is immediately clear that there are certain pros and cons associated with the application of each form. Each of the four primary forms of preaching works to ensure that the parishioner can gain meaning through increased biblical understanding. In order to determine which form of preaching is the most effective, an understanding of the positives and negatives associated with each form is necessary. That will help us fully appreciate what the best forms are for communicating the truth of the gospel.

Positives:

Exegetical

Exegesis means to draw out the true meaning of the text as the inspired author intended. An exegete is one who analyzes the text carefully and objectively and who builds upon sound hermeneutical principles. Exegesis itself incorporates a study of individual words, their backgrounds, their usage, their synonyms, their antonyms, and their figurative usages. Along the way, how the words are organized in sentences and paragraphs, or the syntax of the text, provides an understanding of the train of thought that the Spirit intended. The exegetical form of preaching allows only the message of the text to come out in the sermon. The focus of the sermon is the delivery of the Word of God to the congregation without any extraneous information, or without anything that could detract from the message. It involves the Word of God being conveyed to the congregation without glitz, glamour, pomp or circumstance. It is one of the purest forms of preaching. The preacher reads and sections off the text grammatically as part of the exegesis and relies on the historical background of each book.

A well-crafted sermon written within the form of exegesis has the potential of destroying an objective reading of the scriptures. Other sermon forms have the potential to allow culture to dictate scriptural interpretation. Yet if each culture or generation formulated its own standards of interpretation, the Bible could be reimagined as something necessary only for isolated situations. Its cultural or generational meaning could stray far from what the Word really means and says. What the original recipients of the documents would have understood the text to mean would have morphed into something unrecognizable by either its authors or recipients, making the documents irrelevant. Looking at the text with the mind of an exegete allows the hearer to have a text highlighted and explained with little variance from the text, thus keeping the Word of God as close to what was originally intended.

Exhortative

Exhortative preaching is very interactive. Although listed separately here, the exhortative form can be included with other preaching forms. It is conceivable to develop a message with a primary purpose of urging listeners to be more committed to God and His Word that may include some, all or none of the other forms of preaching. This form of preaching is convictional and appeals to the heart. Exhortative preaching is an enthusiastic discourse based on the Scriptures that urges congregants to make life change. An exhortative message is generally followed by an altar call or some other response method. Exhorting preachers always preach for a decision.

An exhorter wants you to act. E. K. Bailey preached a sermon at Solid Rock Baptist Church in Port Arthur, Texas entitled, *And We Know*, which was an exhortation hum, call and response sermon. This sermon was addressed to a specific congregation and intended to give them a sense of hope and encouragement after they lost possession of their church building due to poor stewardship. As they found themselves facing the task of fundraising to build a new church, Bailey was urging the members of Solid Rock to respond by renewing their commitment to finish the task of rebuilding the ministry.

The exhortative preaching form is highlighted in the book *Doctrine that Dances*.[35] Dr. Robert Smith discusses different preaching methods, and while he does not deal with all forms of preaching, he does explore the expository and exhortative elements of a sermon. He explains the exhortative elements by using musical terminology. According to Smith, improvisation, an integral part of jazz music in which the final form of a musical piece of work is being created as it is being performed, is also used in exhortative preaching.[36] There are not set rules for improvisation, except for knowing there must be substance and a clear understanding of the work (or music or sermon) as it is written. Smith suggests that when preaching happens without substance, the improvisation is meaningless.

When utilizing this form of preaching, the preacher must make necessary adjustments to communicate the Word of God even as the proclamation is occurring. As he is preaching, the preacher begins to retrieve Scripture, experiences, and illustrations that help communicate the Word of God. In the African American church, this improvisation is called a *whoop* or *tuning up*. Smith made a relevant analogy about the value of the content of improvisation. "It can be gourmet, like Maggiano's, or the Olive Garden; it can be the regular Franco American, right out the can; or it can be homemade, right out of mother's kitchen. Regardless, all spaghetti has basic irreducible components. All spaghetti looks like spaghetti whether it has mushrooms and extra cheese on it or not."[37] When the preacher preaches, the basic component is the Word of God. There may be variations in delivery, lecture, whoop or tone, but the proclamation is still the Word of God. The improvisation does not affect the declaration or proclamation of the Word of God.

Exhortative preaching has existed in the African American church for generations. Evans E. Crawford examines the exhortative form of preaching in his work, *The Hum: Call and Response in African American Preaching*.[38] He places emphasis on the importance of timing, rhythm and cadence in the African American context. In requiring the congregation to participate in the sermon, the preacher is both ensuring that the audience remains engaged, and that the audience participates through the use of active listening skills. If the participants are not actively listening to the sermon, their lack of participation would be noticed immediately. The social stigma of not participating ensures reciprocity which potentially increases the dissemination of biblical knowledge and literacy.

Textual

Textual preaching dominated the homiletical landscape in the latter half of the 1800s and the first half of the 1900s. In some circles, it remains popular today. In textual messages, the sermon's structure takes its cue from the biblical text. Both the topic and the main points come from ideas in the text, usually a verse or two, and then are developed by the preacher from other biblical texts. While the length of a passage preached does not define the form of sermon preparation, the typical textual sermon is based on shorter passages. A textual sermon will take its leading ideas from the text and then look elsewhere in Scripture for its development.

Textual preaching provides an efficient way to explain some of the Bible's grand themes (such as Romans 12 and Hebrews 12). They break down some of the larger passages and help give explanation to some of the Bible's foundational concepts. Textual preaching can highlight Scriptural passages that believers should memorize to have easy access to when they need them. Since the text is usually short, it is typically easier to remember and memorize. Textual preaching is also an effective way to preach to non-believers. Bringing the actual words of God to the people gives divine authority to the message. Or for those who have not developed the ability to stay focused for long periods of time, a Scripture passage can be easily understood and remembered by parishioners because the passage a textual preacher uses is usually one or two verses long. Textual preaching has an impact, but ultimately yields less authenticity than expository preaching.

Expository

Expository preaching involves the comprehensive explanation of Scripture. It represents the meaning and intent of a biblical text, providing commentary and illustrations to make the chosen passage applicable and understandable to the parishioner. The word "expose" is the root of exposition, and by definition, explains that the preacher's goal is to take the verses within a passage and expose the meaning of that section of Scripture. As has been stated throughout this book, expository preaching has many benefits. The theological message of the text is clearly conveyed, which serves to increase the biblical literacy of the congregant. The preacher can then use the message as a way of leading the congregant to a deeper understanding of Scriptures. This works to drastically improve biblical literacy, as the individual is not simply told the meaning, but is instead allowed to find it for himself through a teaching-learning experience.

Personal bias of the preacher is understood and mitigated, increasing the connection of the individual to the Lord. The connection is focused on the Word of God and not swayed by the potential benefits to the preacher or the church. A preacher implementing this form to its fullest creates smooth transitions within their sermons to increase the parishioners' ability to understand the message. Persuasion is an important part of this form of preaching. It is applied to ensure that the message remains both pertinent and relevant to the listener. The goal of the message is to persuade the listener to rely on faith and obedience to the Bible. If the expository form of preaching is effectively and appropriately employed, this is a natural byproduct.

In spite of the large number of positives for each of the different preaching forms, there are still certain negatives. An understanding of the limitations of a given preaching form is just as critical as an understanding of the positives when determining the most effective form to use. Without understanding both the positives and the negatives, a pragmatic determination cannot be made.

Negatives

Exegetical
Exegetical preaching focuses on the meaning of sections of Scripture in the immediate context. In the exegetical form of preaching, the congregation is typically presented with an explanation of the text as it was originally intended. Because there is no application of the text, it may be argued that such a form of preaching is not as effective as expository preaching. Exegetical preaching is a simple presentation of the text without a more modern application of the text that can be utilized today. This lack of additional explanation reduces the probability of finding relevancy in the message, and thus makes it difficult for the congregant to apply the message of the sermon within the context of his or her life.

While one of the positives of exegetical preaching is that it conveys the message in a no-frills manner, that feature also serves as a detriment. By removing frills or additional information that may illuminate the text, it becomes easy for the individual to become lost, to misunderstand or to misinterpret what is presented. If he does not understand the information being conveyed, or if he is unable to find the relevancy to his life, he will dismiss the information, turning his time and attention to other pursuits. There is no spiritual growth when individuals are not encouraged to apply the truth.

Another area where lack of understanding is a concern is when preachers share their raw exegetical data from the pulpit. A preacher's initial impulse may be to share with his congregants the data that he has discovered, even though few people in the audience will have a sufficient background to allow them to understand this kind of raw data. The root meanings of words, the translation of ancient languages, the statistics discovered in the exegetical process should all be adapted to suit the vocabulary, education and interest level of the congregants. While the preacher may be a specialist on the verses being taught, he must explain the text in a way that is true to the text but also interesting to his people.

Exhortation

Exhortation preaching requires the congregation to participate in the sermon. The problem surfaces when the individual becomes so caught up in his participation that he fails to truly grasp the significance, culture, grammar and application of the message being conveyed. This form of preaching can partner with expository preaching, but in many congregations, it stands alone. In his work, *Celebration and Experience in Preaching,* Henry Mitchell calls the exhortative form of preaching the emotion, timing, and celebration.[39] The text is read and briefly explained, but there is no application before the hum, call and response. Exhortative preaching can be coupled with exposition to present the text in an exciting manner and to make it more effective and applicable. Exhortative preaching partnered with expository preaching enables the preacher to flow naturally, sermon-izing a text with melody. Another possible drawback occurs when the melody overpowers the preached word to the point that some parishioners are unable to understand what is being said. This often happens when the delivery becomes over-emotional.

Textual

Textual preaching is often criticized as being a flawed area of study and application, because the focus is placed on the human as opposed to the spiritual. This potentially detracts from the ability to teach and convey the Word of God to the congregant. If total reliance is on the individual, the Word of God will be taken out of context, which could damage its credibility and authority. Textual preaching is also susceptible to misinterpretation due to the small amount of text that used in the sermon. Sermons based on limited text have the potential to alter the author's original intent, distorting the original meaning. C. H. Spurgeon, considered one of the great twenty-first century preachers and known as the "prince of preachers," was par-ticularly adept at this kind of sermon.[40] Spurgeon had a rare ability to deal with text. Often, though, his sermons seemed to employ very lit-tle theological depth, which limited the impact they could have.[41] His sermon archives are full of sermons that are one Scripture texts that can easily be misinterpreted, altering the author's original meanings.

It is also possible that a short text could cause the parishioner to see the Bible as chopped into fragments instead of appearing as a living and complete revelation. By taking a few isolated words out of context, its real meaning and intent cannot be discovered. If texts are selected here and there throughout the Scriptures, they are not likely to impress the hearer with the unity of the Bible as a whole. By tak-ing a few isolated words from the book, the preacher runs the danger of using them in whatever way the preacher may desire. To treat the Bible as a mere collection of texts is foolish and yields no worthy fruit. G. Campbell Morgan said, "There are thousands of people who have been brought up in somewhat close relationship to the Christian church who nevertheless think only of the Bible as a book of texts from which sermons are preached, or which are quoted in proof of some theological position."

Expository

Expository preaching, like all the others, also has a downside. The process for writing such a sermon can be difficult due to its complexity. Crafting such a message effectively requires inclusion of each of the six components mentioned earlier. Explanation and interpretation, if it neglects application of the text, is not expository preaching. The preacher must be constantly aware of his actions and words, being careful to monitor for bias. Furthermore, the individual who is listening to such a sermon must work to ensure that the application of the message is received in the same manner in which it was presented, without personal bias or gain. This can be difficult because the very nature of humanity, which is primarily concerned with survival, ensures that the self remains primary. Life, however, is about more than simple survival, and the individual must take extra care to ensure that he has done more than just listen to the message. He must be working to actively apply the context of the information to his life.

The preacher's words matter when they speak justice and hope into being, when preachers act as servants to their communities, interceding on its behalf and mediating God's moral, spiritual, and ethical concern for Christian unity. African American preaching is more than an artistic expression. It is foremost an act of worship. It is ministry of spoken and embodied Word in service to the gospel of Jesus Christ for the community. In other words, it is proclamation of good news that *does* something—it names, provokes, encourages, teaches, and inspires faith—on God's behalf. African American preaching uses the power of language and art to interpret the gospel in the context of Black misery and Christian hope.

The church in the twenty-first century is the beneficiary of a rich treasure of Bible teaching, both in print and online. Gifted preachers God has placed in the church have communicated their Biblical interpretations to the benefit of the American church on a weekly basis. In every situation, regardless of the form used, it behooves the preacher to take full advantage of the resources available to them, even if it varies from the form with which they feel comfortable. The responsibility weighs heavily on the preacher, and it should motivate them to continually acquire a more keen mastery of their craft.

CHAPTER 5

E. K. Bailey: Models Multi-Ethnic Preaching

I TIMOTHY 5:17 tells us that a man of God, especially one who preaches the Word, is to be honored. It is my pleasure to introduce you to a man of God who truly deserves honor. He had a hand in re-shaping the landscape of preaching within the church in general, and specifically within the African American church. E.K. Bailey was one of the premiere African-American preachers of the 20th century, and his legacy continues to this day.[42]

I had the privilege of meeting Dr. E.K. Bailey in 1998 as he was holding a revival in Oklahoma City, OK. Dr. Bailey was at the height of his ministry as I was still trying to plot my path in life. I knew where I wanted to go, but I hadn't planned how to get there. Dr. Bailey sensed that and told me very directly, "If you don't have a plan, it's now time to start planning for future ministry." As we visited, he offered me several recommendations for a meaningful ministry that served as a launching point for my journey into fulltime preaching.

One thing I recognized during our initial interaction was that Bailey was an avid reader. He impressed upon me that being well-read was a necessity. He asked me several questions: "What author are you reading?" "Where did the author go to school?" "What are your plans for ministry preparation?" During this encounter, an interest in preaching was kindled and I began to study the preaching form that he recommended. Bailey so encouraged and inspired me that I enrolled in school. I desired to be faithful to the Biblical text as he had taught and modeled.

I was blessed to have experienced firsthand Dr. Bailey's unwavering passion for preaching the Gospel; however, for those who didn't have the honor of meeting him, his influence still speaks for itself. Bailey influenced thousands of pastors through his untiring effort of research and writing. Noted pastor and author H. B. Charles Jr. said, during a *Cutting It Straight Expository Preaching Conference*, "Thank God for the ministry and the legacy of Dr. E.K. Bailey. His ministry has impacted the lives of countless preachers and will forever be a memorial to those in the African American church that make a commitment to biblical exposition."[43]

Biography

Dr. E.K. Bailey was one of the most celebrated preacher/pastors of my generation. Born on December 19th, 1945, he was the second son of Dr. Vivian Moses and Victoria Bailey. His father was a well-known Baptist preacher who, in 1958, organized the 7th Avenue Missionary Baptist Church in Oakland, California.[44] He was not the only preacher in his family. In fact, one could say that preaching was in his blood. His father, brother, uncles, and godfather were all preachers. It was the strong and continued presence of such men in his life that pushed him toward the pulpit. His parents divorced when he was a child, and because he was close to his father, he chose to live with him rather than his mother.[45]

Four days before the assassination of President John F. Kennedy, his father suffered a fatal heart attack. He was just 45. Not only heartbroken and disconsolate, Bailey also found himself without a home. His father's second wife had never liked him, and following the death of his father, at the age of 17, she turned him out of the house. He wandered the streets wondering what it was that he should do with his life. He found himself on a park bench, and even while he sat crying and lamenting his life and the loss of his father, unable to understand how this was a part of God's plan and how his life had come to this, he was still listening.[46]

It was at this time that he heard his calling. He decided to follow in his father's footsteps by becoming a preacher. In spite of his sadness, he rejoiced at the chance to have a purpose again. He spoke with his remaining family about what he should do to heed his calling. At the behest of his godfather, Bailey moved to Dallas and enrolled in Bishop College. It was here that he pursued his studies. Bishop College provided him with the knowledge and skills that he would need to get his initial start as a preacher. During this time, he also met the woman who would become his wife, Shelia Smith. The two married, and from the life they built together over 34 years, they had three children, Cokiesha, Shenikwa, and Emon. His wife and his children were his constant support through tough times, and they served as his inspiration in both good and bad times in ministry.[47]

In 1975, Bailey founded the Concord Missionary Baptist Church in Dallas, Texas. It became his base of operations. After the founding of his church, he also established a company of his own, E.K. Bailey Ministries, Inc. EKBM was dedicated to creating and facilitating conferences designed to aid others in understanding the word of God and to promote special causes. Bailey believed in his responsibility to change the lives of those who needed it.[48] His church expanded so rapidly that he was able to buy and pay off three mortgages in quick succession. Eventually, he was able to buy a large tract of land. He built his church on that property, where it still stands on a street named in his honor.

Bailey became known for his ability to preach the Gospel. He held a conference in July of 1989 in a hotel ballroom in downtown Dallas where he shared his conviction about expository preaching. His presentation, entitled "Why Expository Preaching?" featured a story from Smithsonian Magazine that highlighted an article entitled *The Moose in Alaska*.[49] Bailey displayed a moose on the screen and expertly juxtaposed the near extinction of the moose with an anemic church that was also facing extinction through attrition of members. Like the moose, preachers were choosing the easy way, leading to death. The presentation, itself an expository sermon, was a milestone at Bailey's conference. He showed how exposition, if done correctly, could strengthen preachers and churches.

In addition to founding Concord and facilitating conferences, Bailey was a renowned author. He wrote *Testimony of a Tax Collector*, *Farther in and Deeper Down*, *The Preacher and the Prostitute*, and *Confessions of an Ex-Crossmaker*. In addition to these works, he also co-authored several books, including *Preaching in Black and White* with Warren Wiersbe. His books are thought-provoking, detailed, and contain the same flair for language and imagery that are present within his sermons. Writing gave him another way to minister to the general public. *Christianity Today* and *Leadership* magazines sought him out to serve on their advisory boards.

E.K. Bailey was intentional to include many preachers who challenged him in his preaching ministry. He wanted to continue crafting excellent sermons by refusing to take the path of least resistance. This path allowed Bailey to study both Caucasian and African American preachers who engaged in expository preaching. While reading pervasively, attending seminary and learning at different conferences, Bailey emerged as one of the leading preachers of the 21st Century. Learning from Criswell, Stott, Vines, Smith and Massey, Bailey created a conference that produced a preaching model from which many preachers still benefit. The E.K. Bailey Conference has developed into a recognized gathering, teaching the form of preaching E.K. Bailey mastered.

In his spare time, he worked for both the National Baptist Convention of America and the Holmes Street Foundation for Boys. He served as an advisor to the conferences that needed him, and he spoke at those that requested his presence. Even with all that involvement, he was an active participant in the lives of his three children. In short, he lived a very full life. He was driven, always working towards his vision and improving the relationship the general public had with God.

In October of 2003, at the age of 58, E.K. Bailey passed away following a third and fatal bout with cancer. Local religious blogger and Dallas Morning News contributor, Rev. Gerald Britt, wrote about Bailey, "He was a generous man, one who freely shared his successes and his failures; his triumphs and his mistakes. He was charismatic, humorous, fiercely curious, and devoted to his family and his church."[50]

Ministry

"Ministry is often examined in terms of who the minister is, not what the minister does. But the vocation to ministry must be understood as a call to identity as well as to practice, one that is rooted in Jesus' life and ministry as well as the Spirit's charisma."[51] While it is important to understand who Dr. E.K. Bailey was, it is equally important to understand what ministry meant to him. Dr. E.K. Bailey was a man who was called to the profession. He felt the Spirit move within him while he was still just a child, and in spite of his age, he trusted in the calling and the resources necessary to ensure that he found his appropriate path in life. The influence of his family served as a means of not only ensuring that he was able to minister to the population at large, but also instilled in him an understanding of what it meant to minister to individuals. Bailey saw the effect preaching could have, and he understood that it was his responsibility to reach out to others and to help them understand the Word of God.

Dr. E.K. Bailey took his listeners farther in and deeper down, particularly in times of trouble. He believed this was his life's calling. Farther in and deeper down was not just a catch phrase, but it described how he attempted to live his life in relation to God's Word. Bailey made this phrase the title of his final book in which he discussed the need for a deeper relationship with God. As Bailey said of his own ministry, "That is what God has called me to do, here and now."[52]

Farther In and Deeper Down may have been the last book Bailey wrote, but the concept was not new for his ministry. He strove to embody that sentiment throughout his career. He was most well-known for his vivid reinterpretations of biblical stories, taking the original tale and presenting it in such a way as to keep it relevant for today's world. Pastor Leonard Leach, who pastors Mt. Hebron Baptist Church in Garland, Texas, was on staff with Bailey beginning in 1979. He observed, "Bailey could take a text and use vivid imagery to get you to understand what he was trying to share in the text. While preaching, Bailey had a commanding presence and a melodious voice. He had a way of drawing you in the text and getting you to see what the text was indicating."[53]

His use of shifting perspectives placed the listener in the shoes of the individual about whom he was speaking. Bailey believed that if people continued to show up and continued to listen to the messages, as long as those messages were biblical and relevant to their lives and their experiences, they, too, would become individuals who loved the Bible. The work of Dr. E.K. Bailey was more than just preaching. It also included ministering to the public, and the effect has been long lasting. Dr. Bailey's message was such that those who heard it continued to heed it long after his death.

E.K. Bailey's Early Preaching

"Preaching is focusing on a portion of Scripture in order to clearly establish the precise meaning of the text, and then to poignantly and passionately move the hearers to adopt the action and attitude of the text."[54] In developing the church's ministry base, Bailey began networking with pastors who were using the multi-staff model. He envisioned Concord's growth and wanted to be prepared to effectively minister to the masses. According to Dr. Major Jemison, Senior Pastor of St. John Missionary Baptist Church in Oklahoma City, Bailey was also impressed with the Southern Baptist ministries of Jerry Vines, Steven Olford, W.A. Criswell, and Paul Powell.[55] After studying Southern Baptist pastors for several years, Bailey started integrating the methods of expository preaching these pastors had been using. He made sure that expository preaching was a priority at Concord.

He was not trying to change the identity of the African American church, but wanted to make sure he offered his church the best teaching and preaching possible.

Due to his fellowship with Southern Baptist pastors, Bailey developed a great friendship with Warren Wiersbe. Bailey & Wiersbe's relationship yielded a book entitled *Preaching In Black and White*. In this book, Bailey discussed the context of black preaching versus white preaching. He stated that the predominant and primary theology employed by African American preachers is that of liberation theology. Bailey indicated that such a preaching form is one that is inherited and he, like other generations had to grow through it.[56] Liberation Theology is a belief held by African Americans that theology is not theology when it does not lift the community of the oppressed.[57]

Through developing relationships with men like Wiersbe and Vines, Bailey had the opportunity to preach to many multi-ethnic crowds. Bailey's preaching faced opposition because he did not allow his message to focus on Liberation Theology. As he transitioned to expository preaching, his message began to have Christo-centric focus. In order to transition to the form he popularized, expository preaching, he knew that attitudes and perceptions had to change.

According to Leach, Bailey did not desire to do church as usual, nor to be limited by the status quo. He organized his newly-formed church with a multi-staff model, which was not the norm for African American churches. He knew that he, himself, was limited, and that utilizing the talents of many volunteers and staff pastors would enhance the reach of his work. He believed that a multi-staff church would enable the church to offer more in-reach and outreach ministries for church members and the community at large. Leach shared that Bailey had communicated that when you had a staff, you were able to offer more availability and services to those who needed you. Pastor Leroy Armstrong, who presently serves as a teaching pastor at McKinney First Baptist Church in McKinney, Texas, was the Executive Pastor of Christian Education for five years under Dr. Bailey. In an interview with Armstrong, he shared that Bailey would, at various times, have over 50 preachers serving on a volunteer basis. As a requirement to becoming a paid staff member, you had to volunteer for an extended period of time.[58]

Both societal issues and his own life experiences had a heavy influence on his sermons. After dealing with the death of his father and working through the tumultuous relationship with his step-mother, Bailey sought counsel from Dr. W.K. Jackson who helped Bailey get on his feet and guided him to Bishop College. Bailey was purposeful in his steps to become a prepared preacher.[59] In the early 1970s, Bailey primarily conveyed his messages through telling biblical stories. He would creatively use metaphors, pictures and skits to teach the text. Bailey's charismatic nature and firm, unwavering belief reverberated through every sermon. For him, there was never any doubt that God had a plan for every individual, and the individual would have that plan made known to him if only he listened. Bailey believed that if an individual attended services, he would become enraptured by the messages and eventually come to embrace the word of God. The person would become a God-fearing individual, one sure of his knowledge in Christ.

On the other hand, it was clear to Bailey that there was a disconnect, and sometimes the message fell flat.[60] While Bailey's personality and natural energy shined through each of his sermons, the narrative preaching style was not as effective as it could have been. Though the stories were being shared with his listeners, they were not able to fully connect with and grasp the sermon's message and application. He did not have as big of an impact as he hoped, and his sermons lacked key elements needed for fully communicating a passage of Scripture. Historical context, culture and literary context studies of the Scripture passage were elements Bailey had yet to incorporate into his sermon preparation and delivery.

According to his widow, Dr. Sheila Bailey, E.K. knew a change was needed to have an impact on his congregation the way he wanted. It was not enough simply to tell the stories of the Bible to congregants; he needed to change his approach regarding crafting his sermons and developing his preaching form.

Transition to Expository Preaching

Bailey believed if people continued to show up and hear the Word of God preached, they would become Bible-loving, God-fearing individuals. He argued that expository preaching challenged the preacher to preach the whole counsel of God. While he recognized that there were many different forms of preaching, after Bailey transitioned to expository preaching, he refrained, in large part, from using any other method.

Bailey's take on expository preaching was unique. He created a compilation of biblical stories interwoven as an expository message, which allowed him to remain grounded in the Scripture. For example, Bailey preached the book of Hosea and incorporated a skit to drive home his point. This sermon was visually arresting, like a Broadway production, and it enabled Bailey to easily explain the text, illustrate the text, and apply the text. This sermon eventually became a book authored by Bailey entitled *The Preacher and the Prostitute*.

Another example of Bailey's preaching was from 1 Peter 5:7 for a sermon called "He Cares." I was fortunate to see Dr. Bailey present this sermon live in Oklahoma City, Oklahoma. He taught it at St. John Missionary Baptist Church where Dr. Major Jemison, one of the hundred plus ministers that Bailey trained and equipped for ministry, was the pastor. This sermon was a collection of calamities that occurred in the Bible. These calamities referenced blind men, the woman with the issue of blood, the woman at the well and a religious leader named Nicodemus. After dealing with all the issues each character encountered, Bailey pointed everyone toward the main theme of the text: Jesus cared. He exposed the text through telling different stories, and used strong vocabulary words and various examples in the modern vernacular to apply the text.

Bailey ushered in a reformation in preaching. As a result of his ministry and his transition to the use of expository preaching, this new form of preaching illuminated the text for the congregation, focusing on the big idea of the text.[61] One of Bailey's sermons entitled "Honor One Another" focused solely on the request, reasons and results of honoring people. The analogy was drawn from Romans 12:10, "Being kindly affectionate to one another with brotherly love, in honor giving preference to one another" about the conspicuous and the inconspicuous parts of the body. Bailey emphasized to his congregants how they should honor one another no matter where or how a person serves in the body of Christ.

Dr. A. Louis Patterson, Jr. of Houston introduced Bailey to expository preaching. Within the African American community, Patterson is respectfully known as the "Godfather of Expository Preaching."[62] According to Dr. Sheila Bailey, E.K. was impressed with Patterson's preaching and sought to learn as much as he could. Bailey, continuously striving for excellence in his preaching, invited Patterson to preach at a revival at the Concord Baptist Church. Bailey's widow recalled, "Dr. A. Louis Patterson, Jr. taught Pastor Bailey [his method] by day, and preached the revival by night." Leach confirmed Mrs. Bailey's memory when he said, "When A. L. Patterson would come and preach, it would be a workshop for us preachers and teachers because of how he would instruct during his preaching. During this time, Dr. Bailey was investing in the lives of the concord Baptist Church as well as his preachers."[63]

Dr. Bailey wanted every minister to be at his best in Christ. He desired for all preachers to be better, and he shared everything that he had to accomplish that task. When Dr. Patterson preached, Bailey would take notes, observe intensely and pay very close attention to him. With the changing of the church and the changing of Dr. Bailey's preaching style, every preacher that served in ministry at Concord examined their own preaching. It was important to Dr. Bailey that everyone listened intently to Dr. Patterson so that they would be able to apply what they learned from him.

Bailey was burdened with a vision of not only numerical growth in the church population, but also spiritual growth of the congregants. He believed that if his congregants truly grew spiritually, the results would have an impact on the community as a whole. His zest for spiritual development led him to recognize that preaching and teaching was a major component of the church's Christian Education ministry. He found that for the church to be genuinely healthy, the church needed good Biblical preaching and teaching.

His vision was to be above average, pressing beyond the status quo and the norm. At that time, the expository method was not commonly used within African American churches in the Oak Cliff area of Dallas.[64] Bailey understood that he preached through the power of the Holy Spirit, and this complete dependency on God ensured that he was in line with God's Word and with the Holy Spirit. The work of the Holy Spirit initiated the transition in his preaching form, and it was God's hand that brought Patterson into Bailey's life to teach him.

While interviewing Dr. Sheila Bailey, she stated that her husband assessed God's deepest desire as being the betterment of the human condition. After witnessing the lasting effect of expository preaching, Bailey chose to preach expository sermons that penetrated hearts and convicted individuals. During his transition to this form of preaching, Bailey took the time to study the craft of expository preaching. He was fascinated by the in-depth learning that occurred through the implementation of this method.

Many of the pastors in the Oak Cliff area of Dallas questioned Bailey about the difference between preaching and teaching. He communicated that preaching puts forth the Word of God, but still has teaching moments that surface therein. Teaching occurs when a learner is informed about a subject matter, granting the learner complete understanding.[65] This is what Bailey sought to do when he switched to expository preaching.

He desired to put forth the Word of God in a manner that would challenge, correct and encourage those parishioners who were listening. Transitioning to expository preaching was not only a means of informing the listener about the message in the text or making the learner more educated, but also a means of inspiring his congregation in their walk with the Lord.

A preacher's goal is to be as effective as possible to ensure that individuals are equipped for effective ministering. (Ephesians 4:11-13, KJV) In transitioning to expository preaching, Bailey had to hone his skill of studying the Bible. John MacArthur Jr. suggests, "Being precise in preaching, hard work is not enough. One must also know how to work in productive study of the Bible."[66] A faithful expositor, one who explains the text well, must be one who understands how to read the text, interpret the text and apply the text. Bailey immersed himself in these elements after his transition to expository preaching.

Preaching After the Transition

Dr. Bailey's early forms of preaching were far different from those in his latter years. In an interview with Dr. Sheila Bailey, she affirmed that her husband had his own unique form, but kept working to be a better preacher and teacher. Ms. Bailey stated that her husband would rehearse his sermons consistently to make sure what he was sharing was substantive. Bailey took great pains to make sure he understood both the Biblical concept and the big idea of the text he was presenting.

Ms. Bailey further contended that her husband spent numerous hours researching history, writing out grammar, checking context and rehearsing his sermons during preparation. Bailey prepared himself because he desired to be an excellent orator, and he sought to become as saturated with Scripture as his father had been. Bailey remembered how his father served, and that example challenged him to work harder at his craft of preaching. The influences of his life served as a means of creating the man who could minister so successfully.

Dr. Major Jemison, Senior Pastor of St. John Missionary Baptist Church in Oklahoma City, considers Bailey his father in the ministry, and with Jemison being a charter member of Concord Baptist Church, he had the unique opportunity to experience Bailey's preaching for years. During my interview with Dr. Major Jemison, he recounted that Bailey believed in searching for stories in the text until he found nuggets. "Every text had a combination, and you had to unlock the combination for the text to come open before the text is ready to be preached."[67] Jemison also observed that Bailey was very vigorous in his biblical studies. He watched Bailey spend thirty to forty hours on his weekly sermon preparation; however, Bailey was also not an originality snob. Jemison stated that Bailey would occasionally use another preacher's sermon or teaching material when he knew that it would bless the lives of his congregation.

Bailey's seriousness and devoutness to the study of Scripture was very evident. In an interview with Pastor Armstrong, he noted that Bailey was one of the hardest working preachers to ever mount a pulpit.[68] Armstrong, during his five years of working for Dr. Bailey, said he witnessed how he would read and re-read the text for hours at a time, getting intimately familiar with and memorizing it. Armstrong said Dr. Bailey felt that it was essential for the text to marinate in your heart before you could share it to penetrate someone else's heart. While reading the text, Armstrong observed that Bailey would engulf himself in the context of the text. Bailey would spend at least a day looking over the setting of the text, studying about the audience for whom the text was written, learning about the customs that would be gleaned from the setting. Armstrong also observed that Dr. Bailey made sure that this time was not rushed, because the context would dictate how the text was exposed. According to Armstrong, another reason Dr. Bailey took his time studying the context was that it would help with application of the text after the exposition was done. Bailey would not have to go fishing for applications, because the context/setting of the text would offer applications.

As a result of his gift, Bailey is considered one of the most influential expository preachers of his time, a title and legacy that continues in spite of his death in 2003. Bailey showed through his life's work that expository preaching provides people with the knowledge and wisdom necessary to ensure their increased understanding of how the Bible is relevant to them today. In so doing, his congregation expanded, the levels of Biblical literacy for the lives of all he touched increased, and most importantly, the closeness between his congregants and God was fostered. Bailey's preaching captivated the African

American church and continues to be a form God uniquely blesses. Churches with pastors that have taken the time to learn the form of preaching E.K. Bailey has developed will continue to benefit from his system. In the words of H. B. Charles Jr., "Thank God for Dr. E. K. Bailey."[69]

CHAPTER **6**

The Landscape of the Church Today and the Future

WHEN I LOOK out over the landscape of where the American church is presently, I see a church that is in the process of redefining itself. Its philosophy and methods, ideas of what church should be, and even what a gathered church looks like are all in radical transition. Churches have had to morph over the years to keep up with a changing congregation. The inundation of all things electronic has created a noticeable difference in the attention spans of people. Media has encouraged and catered to that change by the onslaught of reality TV and fast-paced sitcoms and dramas. The church has found that they must exert an effort to get the attention of people through shifting how they preach and teach the Word of God.

The church is also challenged by needing to communicate with multi-generations within one service. Trying to connect with Millennials, Generation X and Baby Boomers at the same time is exceedingly difficult. Each generation has different motivating influences, different modes of thinking and processing information, and different attention spans. It is difficult to be able to reach these people groups at the same time. It seems that a great many sermons are losing their connectivity due to the way they are communicated. Too many preachers attempt to focus too strongly on trying to be relevant, and subsequently, the content of the message suffers.

After looking at the different dimensions of preaching, African American pastors must consider the communication gap and try to fill in the areas in which the church is lacking. With biblical illiteracy being at an all-time high, it is evident that those who serve in the teaching and preaching ministry of the church must strive to be more diligent in reaching the biblically uninformed. There is a demand for biblical exposition in the African American church, as a lack of this type of preaching has caused doctrinal errors. With expositional preaching this can be accomplished and lives can be changed. Richard Mayhue, in his book *Rediscovering Expository Preaching*,[70] argued that if a return to true biblical exposition does not occur, the western world will continue its gravitation towards a valueless culture.

There has also been a shift in expositional preaching that has included a multi-ethnic focus. More African American preachers are serving Anglo churches and Anglo Americans are serving African American congregations. It may vary geographically, but the pattern is present and churches are accepting this shift. This has enabled the church to wrestle with prejudices that have been overlooked for too long.

There is also a shift back to the expositional and exhortative style of preaching. Those pastors preaching this way are intentionally including, at the end of their expositional sermons, a climax with an exhortative close. I had previously believed that whooping was on its way out; however, it looks like whooping/exhortative exposition has gotten a second wind. Whooping has become more recognized, even in Anglo and Hispanic circles where it previously was deemed as non-legitimate form to be used in sermons. While this type of preaching was how the African American ancestors preached, its recent resurgence has included a variety of different ethnicities. This shift in preaching has seemed to have retained audiences, educated the hearers, and grown churches.

If the older preacher Johnnie R. Bradley could give a word of advice to the younger Johnnie R. Bradley, it would be for him to learn, develop, study, and engage in expositional preaching and teaching. Read, research, and immerse yourself daily in expositional preaching and teaching to become a more prepared preacher. Don't depend on others to teach you the method through conferences, but enroll in school and receive the best training that money can buy. Don't allow temporal things such as clothes, shoes, cars, and homes to outweigh your investment in educating yourself on being a preacher/teacher. If you serve faithfully and master exposition, God will supply those needs.

Preaching is not easy. It is challenging from both a mental and physical perspective. Preaching God's Word consistently is a major challenge and a major task. Over the years, the African American church has concluded that she could not stand without authentic teaching and preaching of the Word of God. Through the toughest times African Americans experienced, the Bible provided comfort, direction and peace. It is my hope that preachers study the expositional preaching style, hold themselves accountable to spend the time needed to create quality sermons, accept the shift to multi-generational and multi-ethnic congregations, and that they communicate using multi-sensory methods. If we pastors, who have been charged to lead the Body of Christ into the future, employ these methods, we will be taking huge strides down the right path.

Sermon Outline Examples

The Mind of Christ
Philippians 2:5

*Textual:

"the mind of Christ" (Phil 2:5)

1. To have the mind of Christ we should pray.
2. To have the mind of Christ we should read the Bible.
3. To have the mind of Christ we should love others.
*Note that the phrase "mind of Christ" is the only content taken from the text. The points are biblical but not necessarily located in Philippians 2:1-11.

*Exegetical

1. Paul encouraged the church at Philippi to be united.
2. Paul warned the church against selfish ambition.
3. Paul shared with them the humble example of Jesus.
*Note that all of the points focus on Paul and Philippi, they do not make contemporary application.

*Exhortative The exhortative form is more audible whooping the Scripture passage after explaining the text.

*Expositional *Big Idea- Shiloh Missionary Baptist Church should follow the example of Christ and display unity by setting aside selfish ambition.

1. Setting aside selfish ambition by submitting
2. Setting aside selfish ambition by serving
3. Setting aside selfish ambition by sacrificing

Recommended by God
Job 1:1-22

Textual Sermon:
1. Job was a perfect man
2. Job was a family
3. Job was a rich man

Exegetical Sermon:
1. Job was from Uz
2. Job's credibility was under interrogation
3. Job did not understand what was going on

Exhortative: Recite all the occurrences in Chapter 1 in chronological order
1. Job was a blameless man
2. Job was a man shunned evil
3. Job was rich
4. Job worshipped God
5. Job was recommended by God
6. Job was accused by Satan
7. Job lost all his possessions
8. Job lost his children
9. Job came in this world with nothing and will leave this world with nothing

Expository: **Big Idea-** Why Bad Things Happen to Good People
1. Job loved God no matter what he had
2. Job trusted God no matter what he experienced
3. Job waited on God even when he did not understand

Application: We must love, trust and wait on God despite the bad things that happen to Good people.
*Good people lose their marriage
*Good people experience financial poverty
*Good people experience death in their families
*Good people get sick
*Good people have difficult assignments

Bibliography

(Endnotes)

1   Hinks, Peter P. *To Awaken My Afflicted Brethren: David Walker and the Problem of Antebellum Slave Resistance* (University Park, Pa: Pennsylvania State University Press) p. 193.

2   http://www.pbs.org/godinamerica/black-church/

3   http://www.pbs.org/godinamerica/black-church/

4   Porter, Dorothy B. *Early Negro Writing, 1760-1837* (Boston, MA: Beacon Press,1971) p.467

5   Lockard, Joe. *Antislavery Literature Teaching Guide: Early African American Antislavery Sermons*. Arizona State University, December 2006. p. 6

6   Henry H. Mitchell. *Black Preaching*. 1979. Harper and Row. 13.

7   Blake, John. *Black preachers who 'whoop' –minstrels or ministers?* 2010. CNN

8   http://www.pbs.org/godinamerica/black-church/

9   Henry Mitchell, *Black Preaching: The Recovery of the Powerful Art* (Nashville: Abingdon, 1990), 13.

10   O. C. Edwards Jr., *A History of Preaching* (Nashville: Abingdon Press, 2004), 3

11   John R. W. Stott, *The Preacher's Portrait* (Grand Rapids: Eerd-mans, 1961), 30-31.

12   Henry Mitchell, *Black Preaching: The Recovery of the Powerful Art* (Nashville: Abingdon, 1990), 13.

13   Ramesh Richard, *Scripture Sculpture: A Do It Yourself Manual for Biblical Preaching* (Grand Rapids: Baker Books, 1995), 23.

14   Phillips Brooks, *Lectures on Preaching* (New York: E. P. Dutton and Company, 1877), 5-6.

15   Greg Heisler. *Spirit-Led Preaching: The Holy Spirits Role in Sermon Preparation and Delivery* (Nashville: B&H Academic, 2007), 31.

16   Ed Stetzer: *Biblical Illiteracy by Numbers.* Christianity Today Magazine, October 17, 2014 edition.

17   G. Anderson, "Part 1: Systematic Theology, Church History and Practical Theology," *The Decennial Publications* 1, vol.3 (1903): 7, 11, 15.

18   Haddon Robinson, *Biblical Preaching: The Development and Delivery of Expository Sermons* (Grand Rapids: Baker Book House, 1980), 30.

19   Knight, G. W. (1992). *The Pastoral Epistles: a commentary on the Greek text* (p. 444). Grand Rapids, MI; Carlisle, England: W.B. Eerd-mans; Paternoster Press.

20   Mounce, W. D. (2000). *Pastoral Epistles* (Vol. 46, pp. 572–573). Dallas: Word, Incorporated

21   *Merriam Webster: Exposition http://www.merriam-webster.com/dictionary/exposition*

22   Robinson, Haddon. *Expository Preaching*, 43

23   Mayhue, Richard. *Rediscovering Expository Preaching*, 1991, 109.

24 McDill, Wayne. *Seven Qualities of Expository Preaching.* 2014 http://www.lifeway.com/pastors/2014/01/08/seven-qualities-of-expository-preaching/

25 Ibid.

26 Richard, Ramesh. *Scripture Sculpture: A Do-It Yourself Manual for Biblical Preaching* (Grand Rapids: Baker Books, 1995), 26.

27 Ibid.

28 Pattison, T. Harwood. *The Making of the Sermon: For the Classroom and The Study* (Philadelphia: The American Baptist Publication Society, 1941), 35.

29 McDill, Wayne. *Seven Qualities of Expository Preaching.* 2014 http://www.lifeway.com/pastors/2014/01/08/seven-qualities-of-expository-preaching/

30 Pattison, T. Harwood. *The Making of the Sermon: For the Classroom and The Study* (Philadelphia: The American Baptist Publication Society, 1941), 35.

31 William, Evans. *How to Prepare Sermons* (Chicago: Moody Publishers, 1964), 37

32 Ibid.

33 Thomas, Robert. *The Relationship Between Exegesis and Expository Preaching,* 1991, 181. Accessed October 18, 2015 https://www.tms.edu/m/tmsj2i.pdf

34 Samuel D. Proctor, The Certain Sound of the Trumpet: Crafting a Sermon of Authority by Samuel D. Proctor (Valley Ford: Judson Press, 1994)

35 Robert Smith, *Doctrines that Dance: Bring Doctrinal Preaching and Teaching to Life.* (Nashville: B&H Academic, 2008), 108, 147-149

36   Ibid, p 148.

37   Ibid.

38   Crawford, Evans E., and Thomas H. Troeger. *The Hum: Call and Response in African American Preaching*. Nashville: Abingdon, 1999. Print.

39   Henry Mitchell. *Celebration and Experience in Preaching*. (Ambingdon Press: Nashville, TN, 2008), 32.

40   Lewis A. Drummond. *Spurgeon: Prince of Preachers*. (Grand Rapids: Kregel Publications, 1993), 13.

41   http://www.spurgeon.org/

42   Croft, Wayne. "E.K. Bailey: Expositor of the Word." *Preaching. com*. 2012, Date accessed March 9, 2016. http://www.preaching.com/resources

43   H. B. Charles Jr., Cutting It Straight Preaching Conference Tribute

44   Ibid.

45   Ibid.

46   Ibid.

47   Ibid.

48   E.K. Bailey. *Farther In and Deeper Down*. (Chicago: Moody Publishers, 2005), Loc 2284-2292, Kindle.

49   www.adn.com/alaska-news/article/moose-deaths-trains-hit-10-year-low-due-light-snowfall

50   Gerald Britt, "Sunday Morning Blessing - Dr. E.K. Bailey," *Change the Wind*, May 2,2010, accessed March 10, 2016, http://www.changethewind.org/2010/05/sunday-morning-blessing-dr-ek-bailey.html.

51   Kathleen Calahan. *Introducing the Practice of Ministry* (Collegeville. MN: Liturgical Press, 2010), 48.

52   Bailey, E.K. *Farther In and Deeper Down*. 2005. Moody Publishers. p. 1

53   Recorded interview with Pastor Leonard Leach, 8/2016.

54   Watson, Maurice. *African-American Preaching in the Context of American Christianity*. 2006. AGTS.edu

55   Recorded interview with Dr. Major Jemison, 6/15/2016.

56   Bailey, E. K. and Wiersbe, Warren. *Preaching in Black and White*. 2003. Moody Publishing. p. 10-11.

57   James Cone. *A Black Theology of Liberation*.

58   Recorded interview with LeRoy Armstrong, 8/12/2016.

59   Dr. Shelia Bailey (widow of Dr. E.K. Bailey), recorded interview by Johnnie Bradley, February 3, 2015

60   Dr. Shelia Bailey (widow of Dr. E.K. Bailey), recorded interview by Johnnie Bradley, February 3, 2015

61   Haddon Robinson, *Biblical Preaching: The Development and Delivery of Expository Sermons* (Grand Rapids, MI: Baker Academic, 2001), 31.

62   Dr. Shelia Bailey (widow of Dr. E.K. Bailey), recorded interview by Johnnie Bradley, February 3, 2015.

63   Recorded interview with Pastor Leonard Leach, 8/2016.

64   Dr. James Mitchell, pastor of Bon Air Baptist Church of forty-two years, recorded interview by Johnnie Bradley.

65   Dr. Shelia Bailey (widow of Dr. E.K. Bailey), recorded interview by Johnnie Bradley, February 3, 2015.

66 John MacArthur, Jr., *Rediscovering Expository Preaching* (Dallas: Word Publishing, 1991), 210.

67 Recorded interview with Dr. Major Jemison, 6/15/2016.

68 Recorded interview with LeRoy Armstrong, 8/12/2016.

69 H.B. Charles Jr., Cutting It Straight Preaching Conference Tribute

70 Mayhue, Richard L. *Rediscovering Expository Preaching.*Sun Valley, CA: Master's Seminary Journal, 1990. Print.

CPSIA information can be obtained
at www.ICGtesting.com
Printed in the USA
FFOW05n1341250917